1e ANNÉE

NUMo 5

DOCUMENTS D'

ARCHITECTURE-MODERNE

ENSEMBLES ET DÉTAILS

FORMES - MATÉRIAUX - COULEURS -

PUBLIÉS SOUS LA DIRECTION DE -

- R - BEAUCLAIR -

- M - J - GRADL -

H - LAURENS ÉDITEUR 6 RUE DE TOURNON

PARIS

ART NOUVEAU
ARCHITECTURE

EDITED BY
R. BEAUCLAIR AND M. J. GRADL

DOVER PUBLICATIONS, INC.
MINEOLA, NEW YORK

Bibliographical Note

Art Nouveau Architecture, first published by Dover Publications, Inc., in 2016, is a new selection of plates from *Documents Architecture-Moderne: Ensembles et Details, Formes, Materiaux: Couleurs,* originally published by H. Laurens, Paris, in 1902.

Library of Congress Cataloging-in-Publication Data

Names: Beauclair, R. (René) editor. | Gradl, M. J., editor.
Title: Art nouveau architecture / edited by R. Beauclair and M.J. Gradl.
Description: Mineola, New York : Dover Publications, 2016. | "Art Nouveau Architecture, first published by Dover Publications, Inc., in 2016, is a new selection of plates from Documents Architecture-Moderne: Ensembles et Details, Formes, Materiaux, Couleurs, originally published by H. Laurens, Paris, 1902."
Identifiers: LCCN 2016020923| ISBN 9780486804552 (paperback) | ISBN 0486804550
Subjects: LCSH: Art nouveau (Architecture)—Europe—Pictorial works. | Decoration and ornament, Architectural—Europe—Pictorial works. | BISAC: ARCHITECTURE / Decoration & Ornament. | ARCHITECTURE / History / Modern (late 19th Century to 1945). | ARCHITECTURE / Interior Design / General.
Classification: LCC NA957.5.A78 D632 2016 | DDC 720.94—dc23 LC record available at https://lccn.loc.gov/2016020923

Manufactured in the United States
80455001   2016
www.doverpublications.com

NOTE

This volume contains fifty-eight plates from a rare architectural portfolio published in Paris in 1902, at the time when the Art Nouveau style—then actually new—was capturing the imagination of architects across Europe just as thoroughly as it was capturing the imagination of poster artists, graphic designers, book illustrators, typographers, and many others. It was edited by two well-known versatile Art Nouveau pioneers, René Beauclair (1877–1960) and M. J. Gradl (1873–1934), remembered today for their work in many areas including ceramics and textiles for Beauclair and typography for Gradl; both were also active jewelry designers.

Designs by a varied roster of contributors from France, Germany, Austria, England, and The Netherlands include the façade of an apartment building, storefronts, window frames, decorative plaques, interiors and individual room designs of many kinds, fireplaces, small houses, railings and gates, restaurants, weather vanes, and many other building and decorative details. Both editors are also represented by individual plates in the collection.

PLATE 1—MAXIME ROISIN, PARIS

Façade of an apartment building.

PLATE 2—ERWIN PUCHINGER, VIENNA

Left: Window section of plaster façade with a stenciled color panel.
Right: Design of a window between pillars. The sculpted plaster façade is enhanced with ceramic tiles.

PLATE 3—MAXIME ROISIN, PARIS

Storefronts. Executed primarily in wood, adorned with sheet metal and wrought iron. The ornamentation is partly carved and partly poché. The awning *(top)* spans the entire width of the store and contains electric light fixtures. The gates *(top and bottom)* can be retracted down into the basement.

PLATE 4—A. LAVERRIÈRE, PARIS

Porches, sculpted and carved stone.

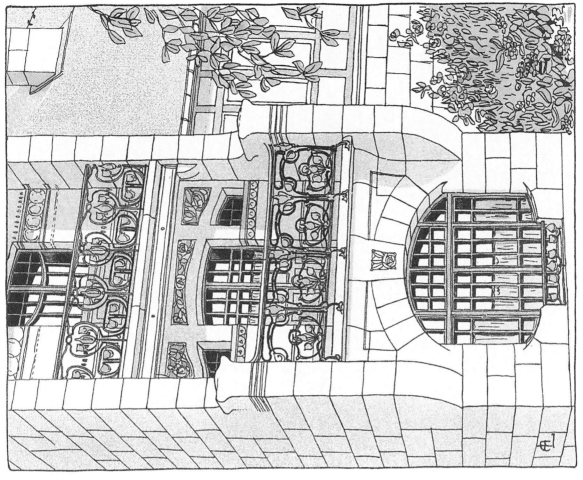

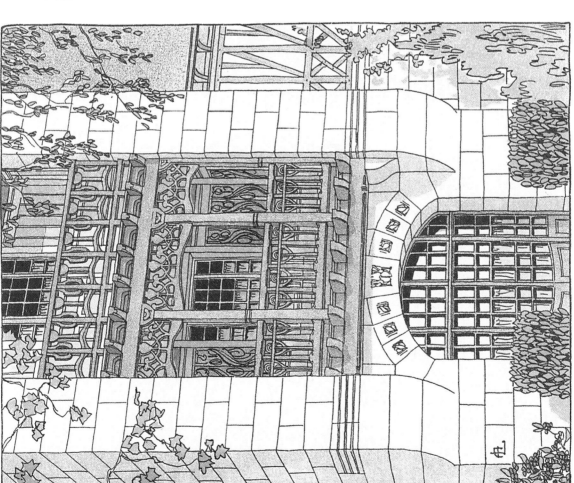

PLATE 5—A. LAVERRIÈRE, PARIS

Left: Balcony of carved wood. *Right:* Balcony in stone and wrought iron.

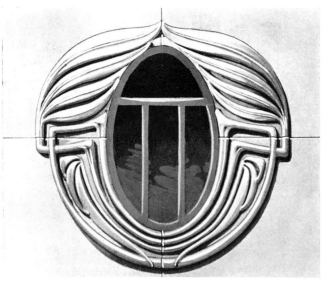
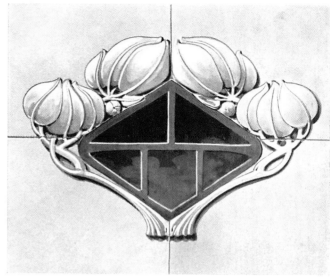
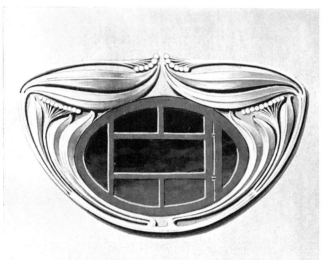

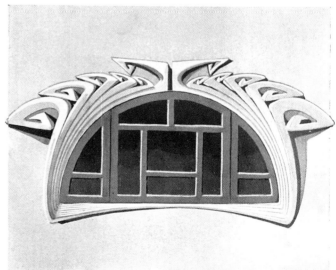

PLATE 6—JEAN DESMOULINS, PARIS

Bulls-eye windows in carved stone.

PLATE 7—JEAN DESMOULINS, PARIS

Window frames in carved stone.

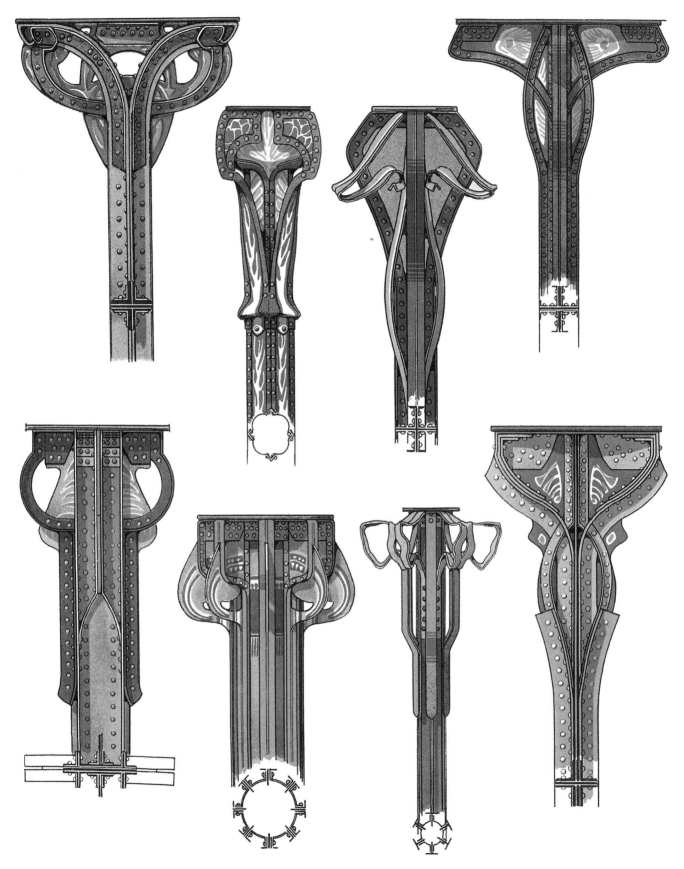

PLATE 8—WILHELM VON TETTAU, BERLIN

Designs for capitals of support columns in iron. The cross sections of these supports, which are all riveted in
different sections, can easily be modified by the elimination of two or three angles.
These capitals call out for a note of strong color.

PLATE 9—PATRIZ HUBER, DARMSTADT

Entry hall.

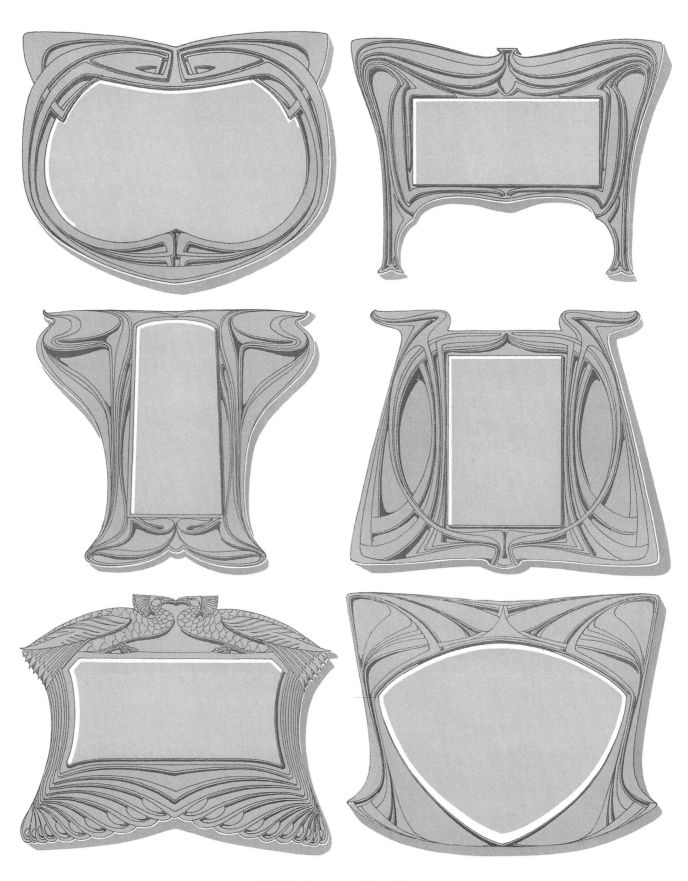

PLATE 10—P. GAUBIL, PARIS

Plaques in carved stone.

PLATE 11—M. J. GRADL, STUTTGART

Columns. *Left to right: (1, 3, 4, 6, 7, 9)* Columns in stone. *(2, 5, 8)* Columns in wood.

PLATE 12—JEAN DESMOULINS, PARIS

Heads and sills of window openings in carved and engraved stone.

 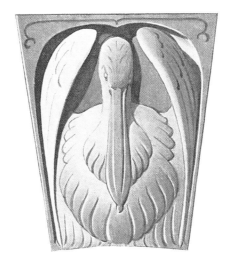 

 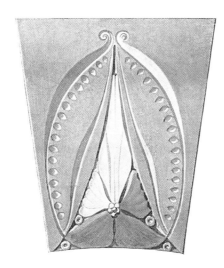 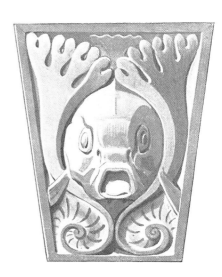

PLATE 13—J. B. HEUKELOM, AMSTERDAM

Keystones in carved stone.

PLATE 14—RENÉ BEAUCLAIR, PARIS

Fireplace wall in a waiting room.

PLATE 15—E. SCHAUDT, BERLIN

Interior of a music salon (window side).

PLATE 16—WILHELM VON TETTAU, BERLIN

Top left: Facing for a skylight, with riveted iron structure clad in copper.

Top right: External view of a dormer window.

Bottom: Iron cupola.

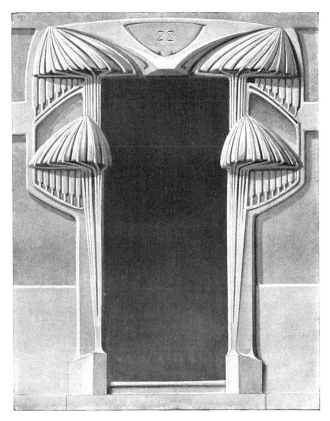

PLATE 17—JEAN DESMOULINS, PARIS

Small side doors in carved and engraved stone.

PLATE 18—HERMANN MAYER, STUTTGART

Buffet in a restaurant.

PLATE 19—MACLACHLAN, STUTTGART

Restaurant interior and buffet.

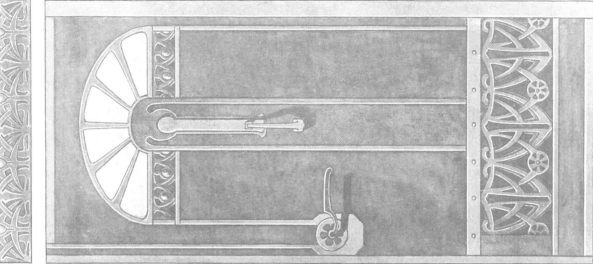

PLATE 20—RUDOLF BOSSELT, DARMSTADT

Entry doors in copper or repoussé sheet metal.

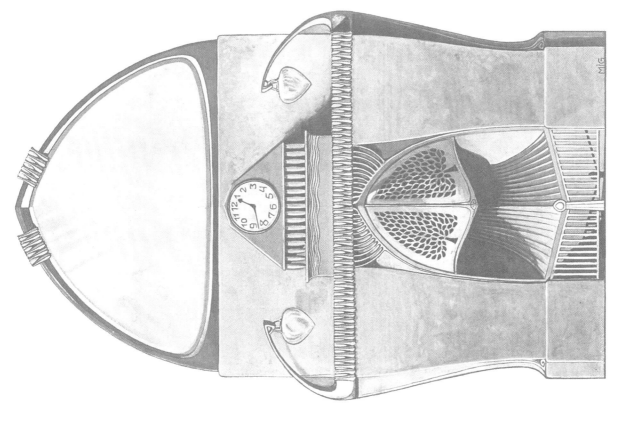

PLATE 21—A. JULLOT, PARIS and M. J. GRADL, STUTTGART

Left: Fireplaces in carved and sculpted stone.

Right: Gas fireplace in marble, with a wood-framed mirror, copper ornamentation, and bronze light fixtures.

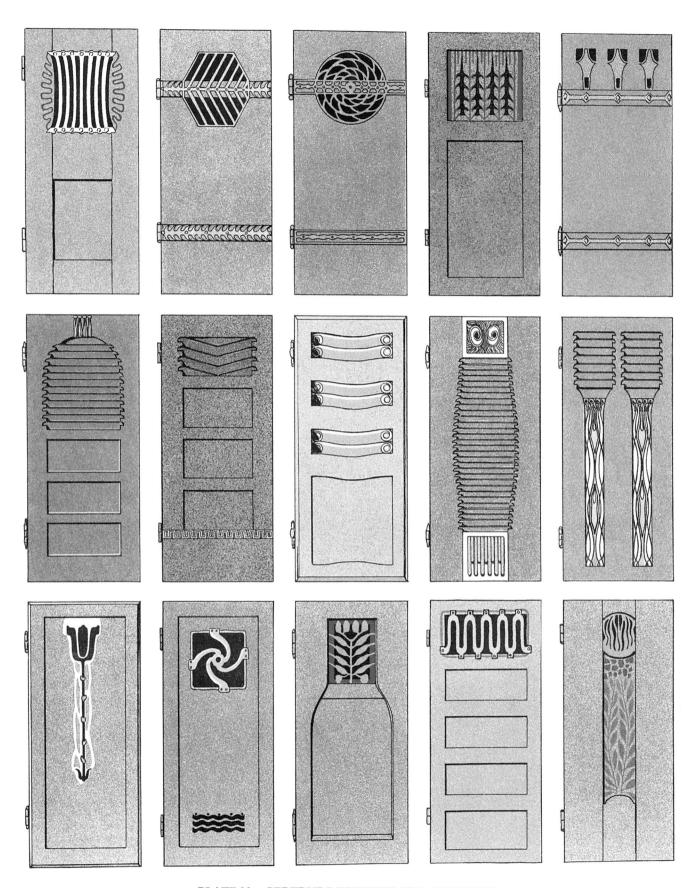

PLATE 22—GERTRUDE KLEINHEMPEL, DRESDEN

Wood shutters with stenciled ornamentation, sculptures, and wrought iron.

PLATE 23—F. W. JOCHEM, DARMSTADT

Small private three-story residence. The ground floor is constructed of limestone;
the rest of the building is brick and faced with ceramic tiles and plaster on the second floor,
and then with tiles up to the roof level.

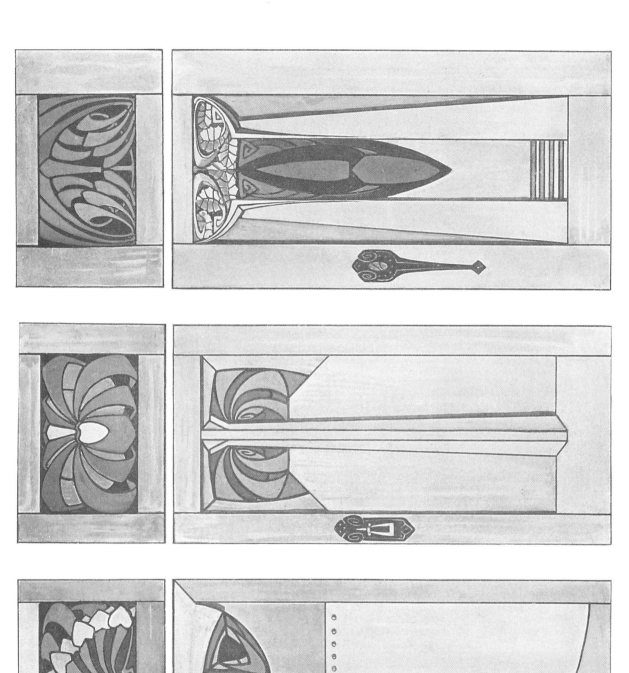

PLATE 24—PATRIZ HUBER, DARMSTADT

Double and single doors with engraved panels and lit with transom windows.

PLATE 25—OTTO BAURIEDL, MUNICH

Basement windows in limestone or concrete. Grilles in wrought iron decorated with plates of riveted sheet metal.

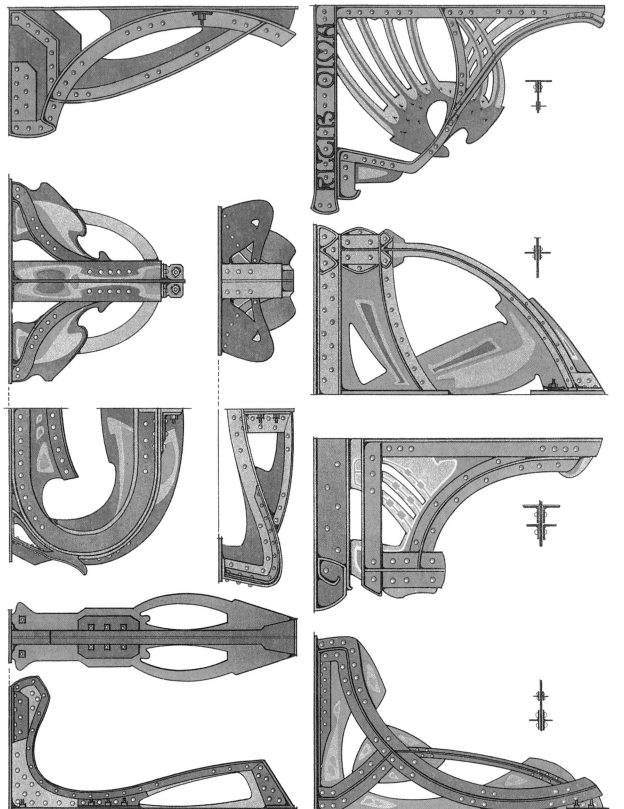

PLATE 26—WILHELM VON TETTAU, BERLIN

Brackets, rafters, and supports in iron.

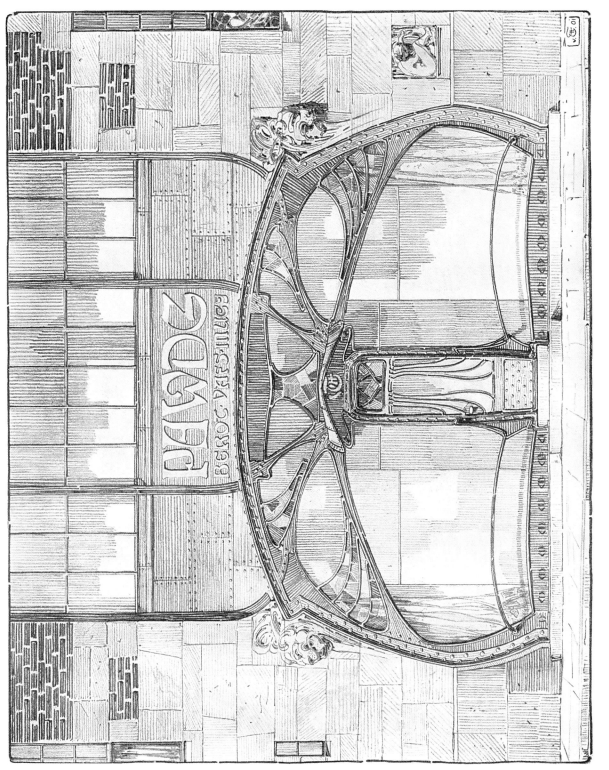

PLATE 27—WILHELM VON TETTAU, BERLIN

Store exterior. Constructed of iron plates. The doors as well as the awning are made of copper.
The windows are divided in half with colored glass.

PLATE 28 — MARCELLUS KAMMERER, VIENNA

From top to bottom: (1) Entablature of a plaster façade with pillars. The cornice rests on brackets extending from the wall. The stucco ornaments are partially gilded. *(2)* Top of a plaster façade covered with copper. The top windows form linked vaults with iron supports. *(3)* Entablature of Monier construction. Window openings are decorated with pieces of colored glass. The curved molding is partially gilded, in imitation of a mosaic. Between the windows there are protruding majolica disks. *(4)* Entablature of a stone façade. The bronze wreaths are enhanced with pieces of blue glass.

PLATE 29—MARCELLUS KAMMERER, VIENNA

Windows of a plaster façade; sculpted and gilded stucco. The lintels of the windows are visible. *Top middle:* Window adorned with ceramic tiles. *Top right:* Lower panel is decorated with a mosaic of colored glass. *Bottom middle:* Window flanked by recessed panels of gilded and sculpted stucco. *Bottom right:* This window is supposed to be part of a monument.

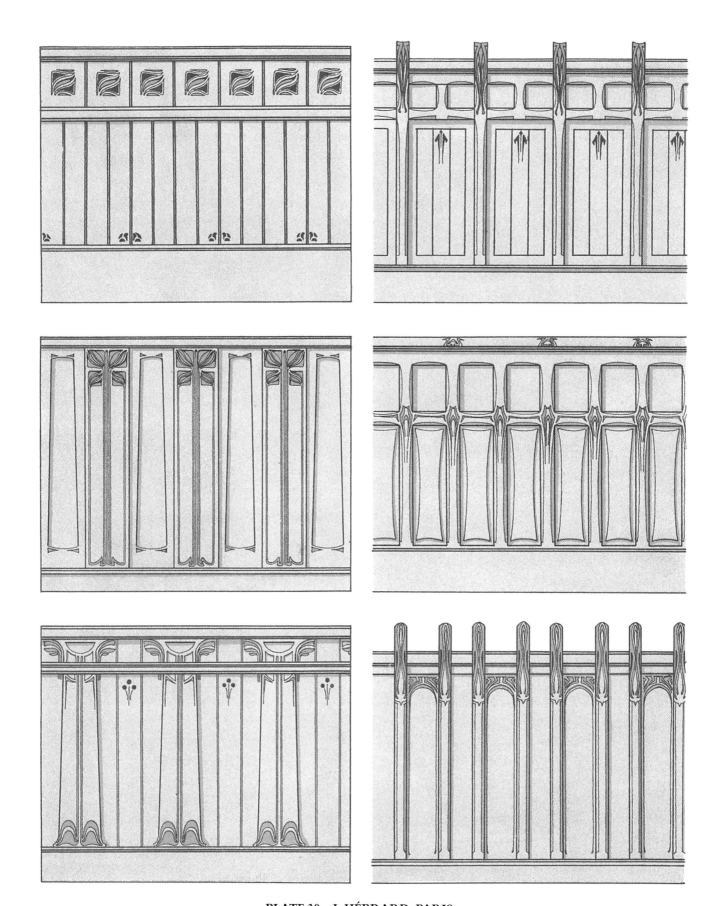

PLATE 30—J. HÉBRARD, PARIS

Wainscoting with carved ornamentation.

PLATE 31—ERICH KLEINHEMPEL, DRESDEN

Gates and doors in wrought iron and riveted and embossed metal.

PLATE 32—E. SCHAUDT, BERLIN

Fireplace in a conference room or public meeting room.

PLATE 33—ELIEL SAARINEN, HELSINGFORS

Living room.

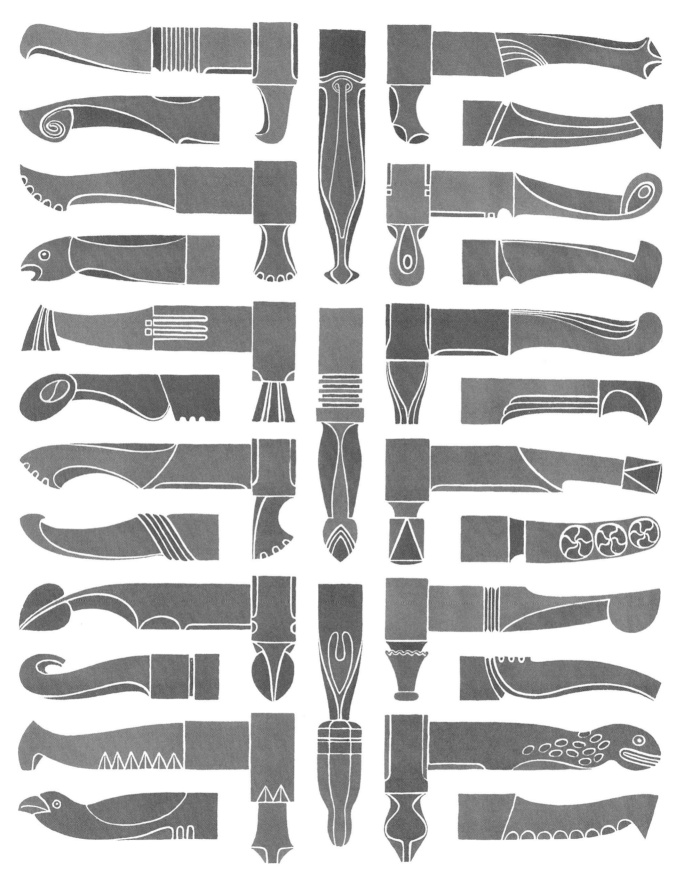

PLATE 34—M. J. GRADL, STUTTGART

Joists.

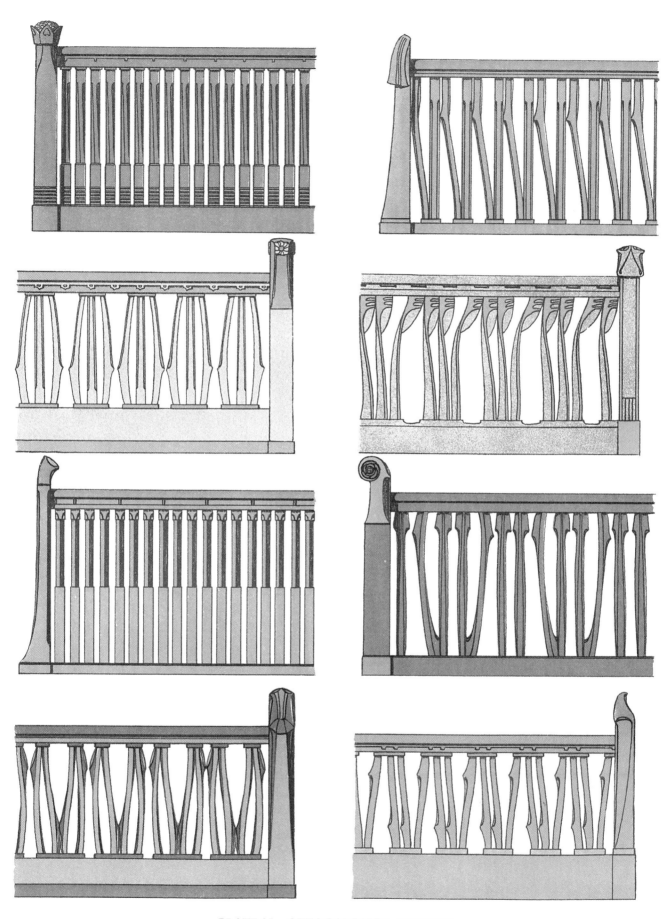

PLATE 35—OTTO BAURIEDL, MUNICH

Handrails in carved and beveled wood.

PLATE 36—MAURICE DUFRÈNE, PARIS

Motifs for sculpted wood: supports, brackets, etc.

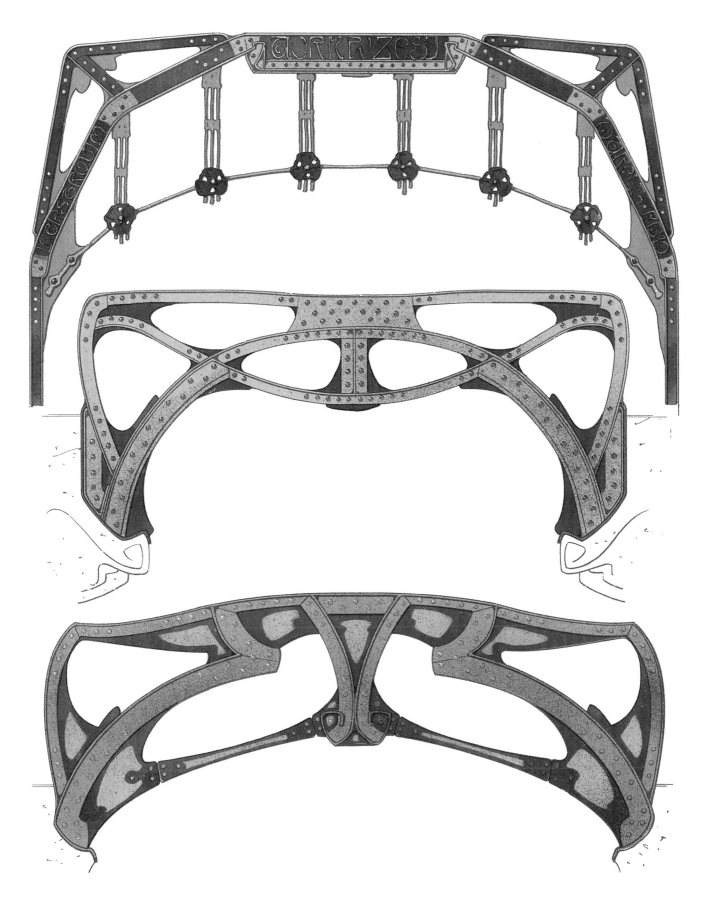

PLATE 37—WILHELM VON TETTAU, BERLIN

Lintels composed of iron shapes with fillets that end in curved tips. When placed on the glass of display windows,
they are finished only on one side; on the other hand, in an open hall, their two profiles are the same.

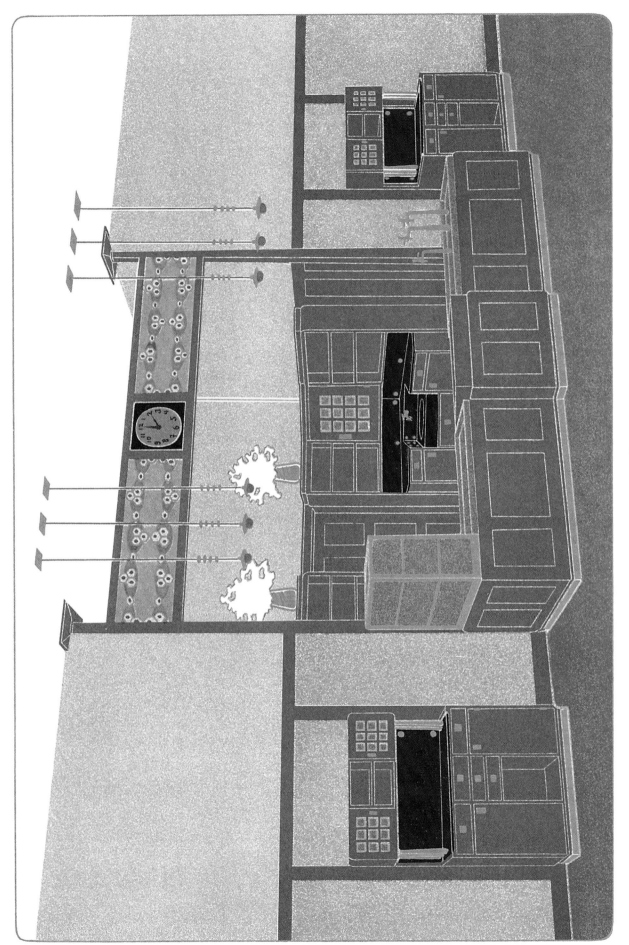

PLATE 38—RICHARD MÜLLER, VIENNA

Buffet of a restaurant.

PLATE 39—FRITZ KLEINHEMPEL, DRESDEN

Buffet of a restaurant.

PLATE 40—M. J. GRADL, STUTTGART

Top: Weather vanes. *Bottom:* Tower finials.

PLATE 41—FRANZ PANKOK, STUTTGART

Staircase and vestibule.

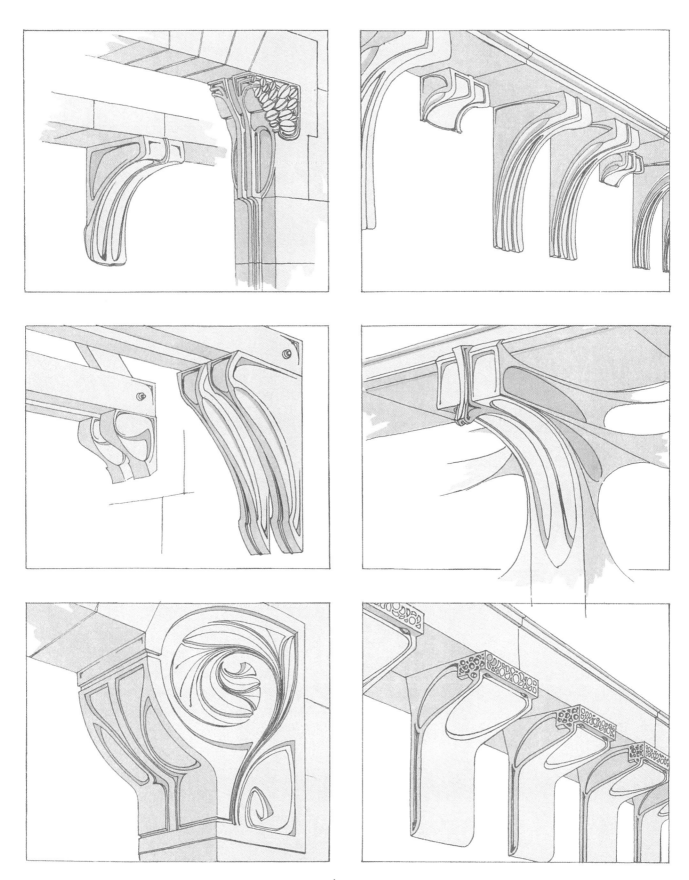

PLATE 42—RENÉ BEAUCLAIR, PARIS

Brackets in stone and stucco.

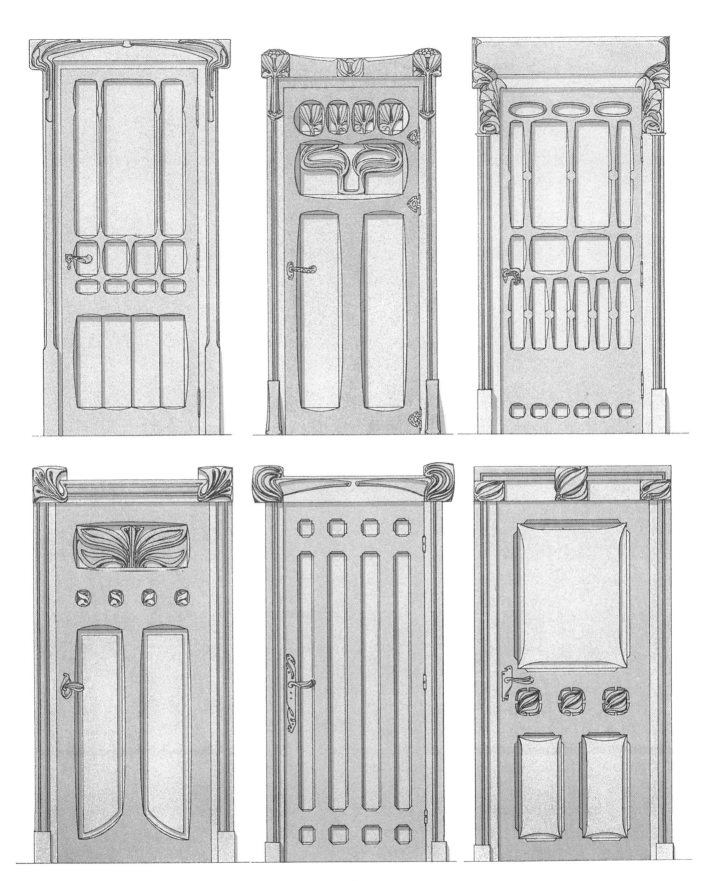

PLATE 43—J. HÉBRARD, PARIS

Carved doors.

PLATE 44—ERICH KLEINHEMPEL, DRESDEN

Top left: Painted exterior door with painted ornamentation; cathedral glass, iron trim. *Top right:* Exterior door with two colors, polished brass trim, mirrored glass. *Bottom left:* Door with two panels, polished, with sculptures, trim, and grille in brass, mirrored glass. *Bottom right:* Glazed door, matte tint, leaded cathedral glass, nickel-plated trim.

PLATE 45—FRITZ KLEINHEMPEL, DRESDEN
Outdoor hall with stairway.

PLATE 46—MAURICE DUFRÈNE, PARIS

Details of railings in wrought iron. *Top row and bottom right:* Garden fences. *Middle:* Balcony railing.
Bottom left, above: Basement window grate. *Bottom left, below:* Window grille.

PLATE 47—J. B. HEUKELOM, AMSTERDAM

Balconies in carved stone with wrought iron railings, front and side views.

PLATE 48—PATTEN WILSON, LONDON
Dining hall.

PLATE 49—PATTEN WILSON, LONDON

Foyer of a theater.

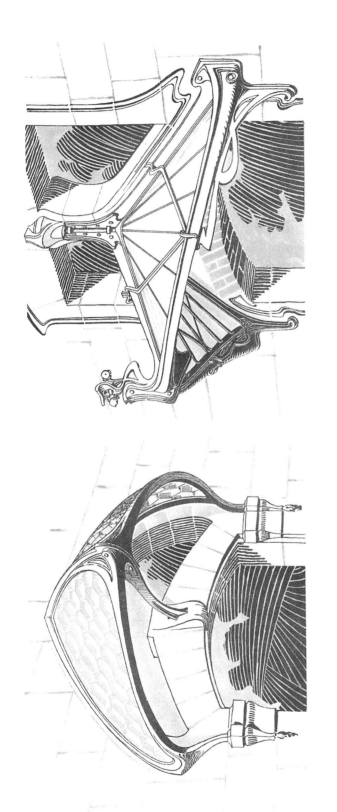

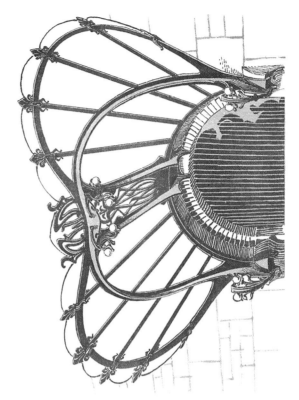

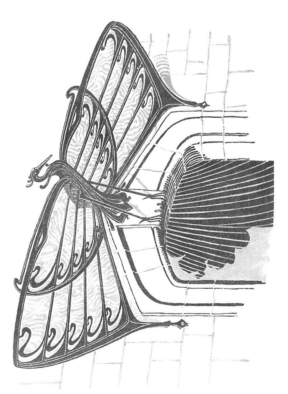

PLATE 50—MAXIME ROISIN, PARIS
Canopies in wrought iron.

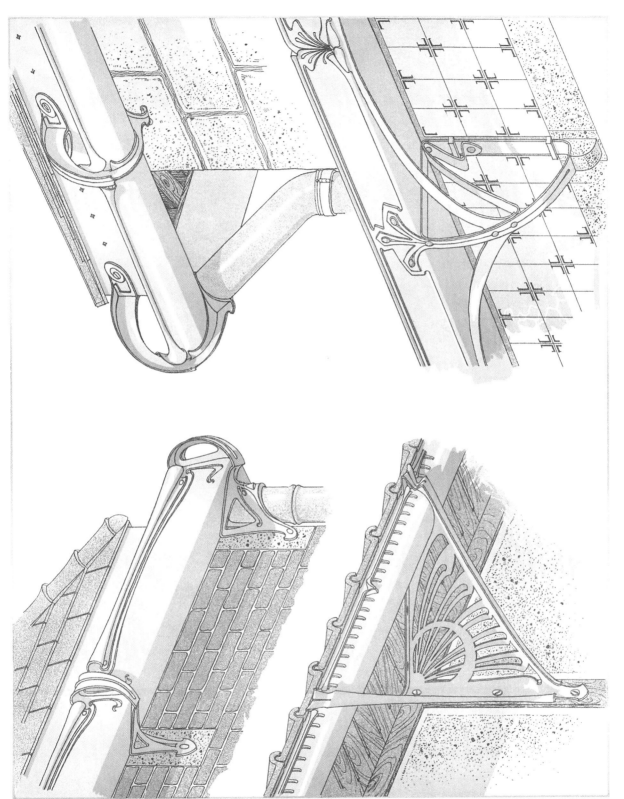

PLATE 51—MAXIME ROISIN, PARIS

Gutters with corner pieces and supports in wrought iron.

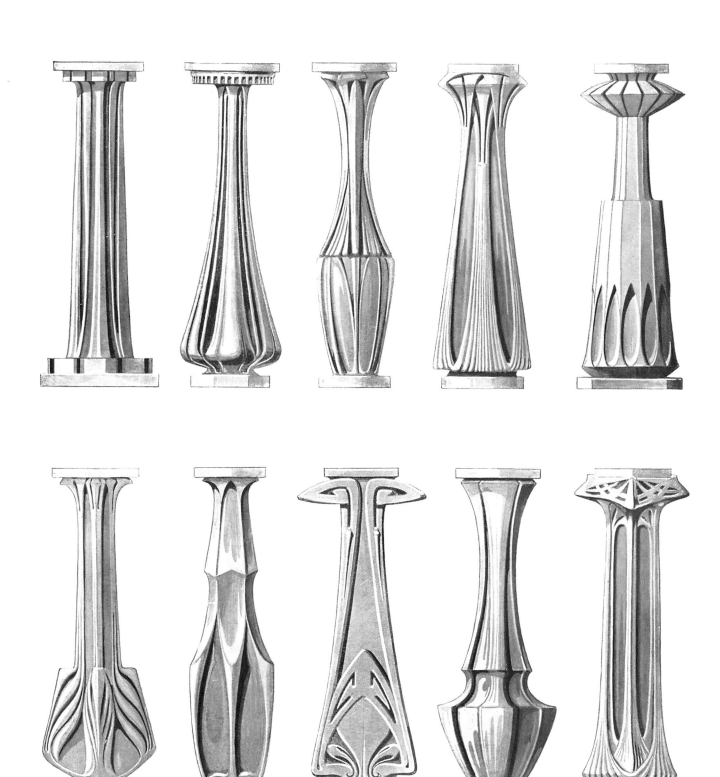

PLATE 52—P. GAUBIL, PARIS

Balusters in limestone or concrete.

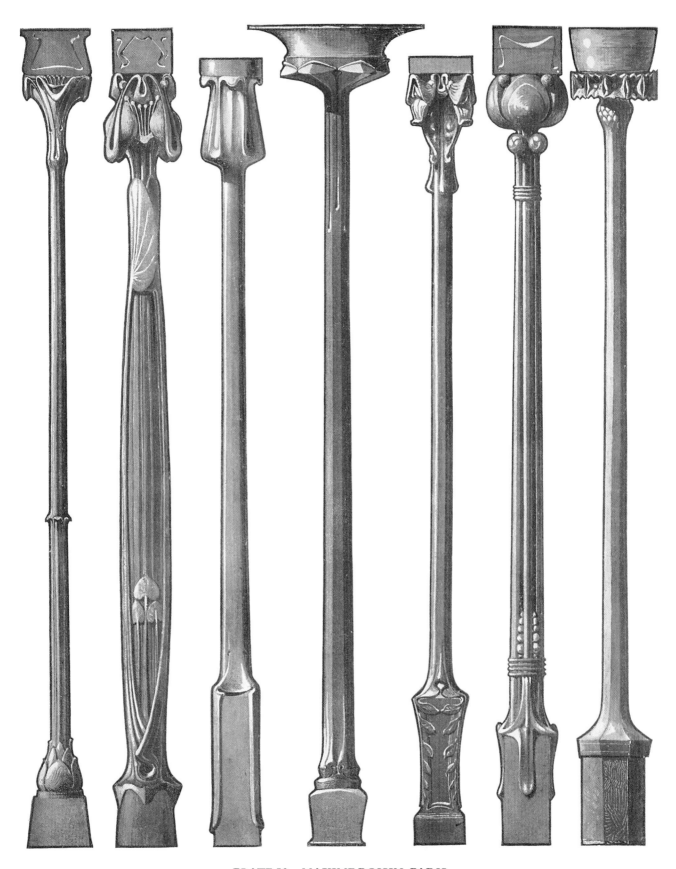

PLATE 53—MAXIME ROISIN, PARIS

Cast iron columns.

PLATE 54—MAURICE DUFRÈNE, PARIS

Details of stone columns; pilasters, balusters, friezes, etc.

PLATE 55—MAXIME ROISIN, PARIS

Balconies of wrought-iron openwork with repoussé and hammered sheet metal.

PLATE 56—PAUL BÜRCK, MAGDEBURG

Mosaic paving.

PLATE 57—VALENTIN MINK, DARMSTADT

Entrance hall.

PLATE 58—MARCELLUS KAMMERER, VIENNA

Corner façade of an apartment building.